Written by Jean-Pierre Reymond
Illustrated by James Prunier

*Specialist adviser: Ian F. Mercer,
Geological Museum, London*

*ISBN 1 85103 031 X
First published 1988 in the United Kingdom by
Moonlight Publishing Ltd,
36 Stratford Road, London W8*

*© 1987 by Editions Gallimard
Translated by Sarah Matthews
English text © 1988 by Moonlight Publishing Ltd
Printed in Italy by La Editoriale Libraria*

POCKET • WORLDS

Metals
and Their Secrets

Metals are born from
the earth and from fire.
 Let us follow their story...

THE WORLD WE USE

Can you see any metals around you?
There are metals everywhere, aren't there? Cars are made of them, locks on doors, the buckles on belts, scissors, knives and forks... More things than you can count. We have come to rely on metals for all sorts of things.

Metal is good at conducting the electricity which keeps our homes and factories working. High-tension electric cables are checked regularly.

How can you recognise a metal?
First of all by the way it shines. Then by the fact that you can't see through it: metal is opaque. It feels cold when you touch it. It is a good carrier of heat. There is only one metal we use which is not solid: the mercury in a thermometer.

There is metal in the food you eat: iron helps to make you strong and calcium builds up your bones and teeth.

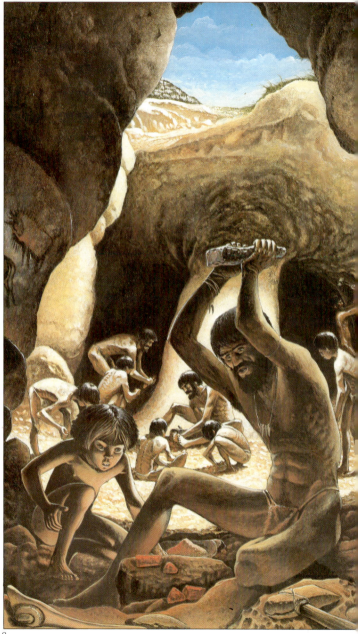

Gold nugget Native silver Native copper

Where do metals come from?

Sometimes you can find pure lumps or 'nuggets' of metal, called 'native metals'. Nuggets were the first metals used by early men. But usually metals are well hidden away in rocks underground. Rocks are made of minerals. Some minerals, with metals in them, have been concentrated together by natural causes – hot water flowing through cracks in the rocks over the years, or maybe a sudden explosion. The rocks that contain these useful minerals can be mined, and are called 'ores'. **The useful minerals are separated from the ores and treated to give us the metals we use.**

By crushing iron ore, which is red, and copper ore, which is green, early men made lovely colours to use in their cave paintings.

The invention of the lost wax technique made it possible to mould metals. A wax model was covered with a clay mould.

The discovery of fire opened up another possibility: people found they could separate, or extract, metals from their ores. By heating the ore with charcoal, parts of the ore were removed, and the metal was released. Extracting metals like this meant not only that people had more metal to make things from, but also that they could use metals they hadn't been able to get at before.

This sword from northern Europe was cast in a mould.

They could pour off molten metal into moulds, to make all sorts of things.

An iron axe-head

Molten metal was poured into the mould. The wax melted and ran away. The cooling metal hardened, and the mould was chipped off.

About five thousand years ago, people began to use two metals mixed together: copper and tin, a soft, grey metal. When they were melted together they made **bronze**, a much tougher metal than either of them had been on its own. <u>This mixture of different metals is called an alloy</u>: combining them increases their hardness and their strength. Using bronze, people made strong weapons, tools and sculptures.

Greek helmet made of bronze

Iron key

You have seen iron: the 'tin' cans food is stored in are made mostly of steel, and steel is mostly made from iron. **There is a lot of iron ore in the ground**. But you need to heat the ore to over a thousand degrees centigrade to get the iron out. Early man did not know how to do this. The iron they used came from meteorites, big rocks which fall to earth from space. Gradually, men learnt to make hotter and hotter ovens for the copper and bronze they used for jewellery, pots and weapons.

The Iron Age

More than three thousand years ago, Hittites in the Middle East began to use furnaces to extract iron from iron ore. Iron was stronger and stayed sharp longer than bronze. The Iron Age had arrived!

This meteorite was found in Greenland. For centuries, Eskimos have used iron from meteorites to make their weapons.

The Hittites put the pieces of broken-up ore into a furnace. They blew on the coals to make them hotter.

The bellows kept the furnace white-hot; the metal was left as a lump mixed with the waste.

A Roman smith with his assistants

A smith works with metal. After the iron has been extracted from the ore, the smith has to beat it hard to get rid of the impurities. Then he heats it in his forge fire. When it is red-hot, he shapes it with his hammer on an anvil. The flat top and pointed, rounded end of the anvil help the smith to shape the metal in different ways, depending upon what he is making. A helper keeps the fire hot with a pair of bellows. Sometimes, after it is shaped, the metal is plunged into cold water to make it harder.

Horseshoes

An 18th-century smith shoeing a horse

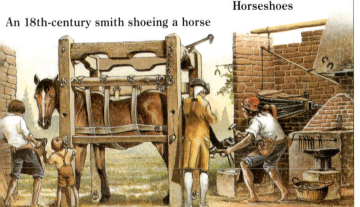

Iron may be the most useful of metals, but **gold is the most precious**. It is very rare: in one tonne of earth, there is on average 35 kilos of iron and one hundredth of a gram of gold. It always gleams and glows, and never grows dim! The Egyptians called it "the body of the gods".

Alchemists in the Middle Ages

Alchemists were half scientists and half sorcerers. They tried again and again to turn ordinary metals into gold – without success! They thought that the seven metals known at the time of Christ came from the seven known planets.

They thought that gold came from the Sun, silver from the Moon, lead from Saturn, and mercury from... Mercury.

Gold   Silver   Mercury   Lead

One of Croesus' coins

Early medieval gold ring

Gold ingot

What are coins made from?
Mostly from an alloy of copper and nickel, a very strong, silver-coloured metal.

Hallmarks on silver

The first coins were made of precious metals: gold or silver. King Croesus of Lydia was the first ruler to have his portrait on a coin. He was also the first to have metal objects stamped with a hallmark; these appear on everything made of a precious metal. The hallmark tells us the quality of the metal, where it comes from, and when it was made.

A silver goblet from ancient Peru

Jewellers have their work hallmarked. Their materials have changed little over the centuries. They work now just as they always have done, using precious metals: gold, silver and, more recently, platinum. They shape them in moulds, or hammer them and engrave them with sharp tools.

Clockmakers make very precise cog-wheels to turn the mechanisms of their clocks. They use hard metals which won't wear out too quickly.

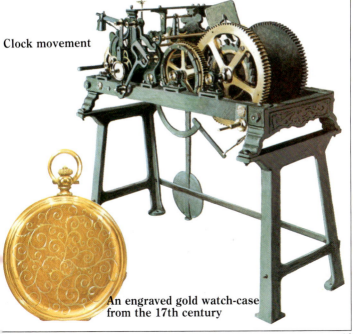

Clock movement

An engraved gold watch-case from the 17th century

The armourer made armour for knights in the Middle Ages. He signed his work with a stamp or engraving.

The coppersmith makes pots and cauldrons, hammering the soft metal around a wooden post.

This locksmith in the 19th century did not only make locks and keys, but also strong-boxes and steel beams.

A cutler in the 17th century. He has made some knives, and now he is sharpening them on a whetstone.

A nailmaker in the 19th century would make all sorts of nails. His dog worked the bellows by running on a treadwheel.

Indian jewellers engrave and chisel designs on the dishes and vases they have made.

Early miners' lamps were oil-lamps; now they use electricity.

Metals have to be dug out of the ground.

The first mines were in the open air, and called open-cast mines. But, as the need for metals grew, the mines had to go deeper and deeper down into the earth. Nowadays, the deepest gold mine in the world is in South Africa. It goes down for more than three thousand eight hundred metres. Working in a mine has always been dark, dirty and dangerous.

Miners go down into the mine early in the morning and stay underground all day long.

This picture shows mines from three different periods: below, in the Middle Ages; above, in the 18th century; and top left, in the 19th century.

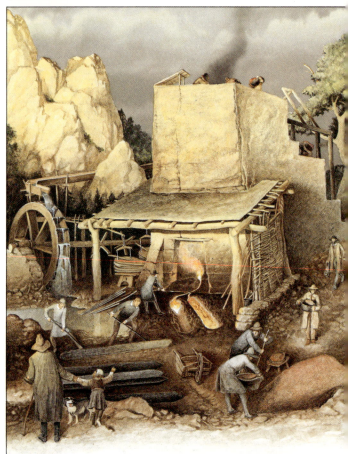

One of the first blast furnaces in Europe: now at last people could heat iron ore to obtain molten iron.

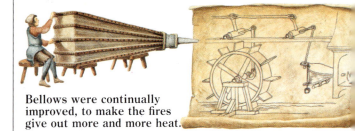

Bellows were continually improved, to make the fires give out more and more heat.

Metallurgy is the study of metals and the art of working them. **<u>Over the last two centuries, several new metals have been discovered</u>**: aluminium, nickel, titanium, uranium, and many others. Aluminium is the second most used metal in the world today, after iron, but it was only isolated just over a hundred years ago. New kinds of power, particularly electricity, made new kinds of treatment possible.

A smith is pouring molten iron in a beautifully-shaped mould of a gate.

Over the ages, smiths learned to make better scythe blades.

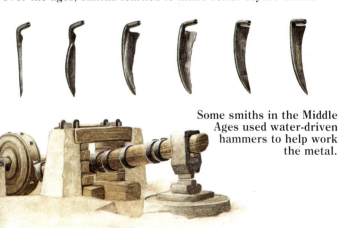

Some smiths in the Middle Ages used water-driven hammers to help work the metal.

The age of steel began in the 19th century.

That is when most of the big steelworks were built.

What is steel? It is a mixture of iron and a little bit of carbon. This makes an alloy which is very strong and long-lasting. Look around you and see how many things made of steel you see: cars, guttering, buttons, posts, pipes, barriers...

By adding small quantities of other metals to the original alloy, steel can be given all sorts of qualities. Stainless steel contains chromium and nickel, which stop it rusting. Nowadays, the use of steel stands as a measure of a country's wealth. The United States use more steel than any other country in the world.

A 19th century steel town

Outside and inside a steelwork

What stages must metal go through before it is made into something?

First of all it must be separated from the ore, then refined, which means made as pure as possible, and then mixed with other metals to make an alloy. After all that, it may be moulded, like the keels of ships, or flattened and run through rollers, like rails and girders, or hammered by power-hammers, or pressed into shape like the bodywork on cars.

Huge rollers flatten and shape the bars and sheets of steel

Thanks to metal, people have been able to build taller and taller skyscrapers.

But they have to be careful to take account of how metal behaves at different temperatures: when it's cold, the Eiffel Tower, in Paris, contracts by ten centimetres!

The Eiffel Tower is made of 15,000 pieces of iron riveted together, with staircases like this inside.

Metals have to be protected: water and salt make iron and steel rust. They have to be painted, or covered with other metals, like chromium, which don't rust.
Some metals have very special uses, like cobalt, which is used in medicine.

The metalwork gleams on this American truck

In America,
Mohawk Indians work
at building skyscrapers,
climbing the iron girders
right to the top. They
have no fear of heights!

Old cars, factory waste, tin cans, broken bicycles The metal they contain can all be used again and again. They are collected in scrapyards, where scrap-metal workers break them up, ready to be recycled. Did you know that almost half the platinum and lead used today has been recycled? Some metal waste is dangerous, though – uranium remains harmful for hundreds, and even thousands of years.

Sometimes fish swallow poisonous metals which have been thrown away by factories. If people eat the fish, they may be poisoned too. To be really safe, we should be very careful what we throw away, and where.

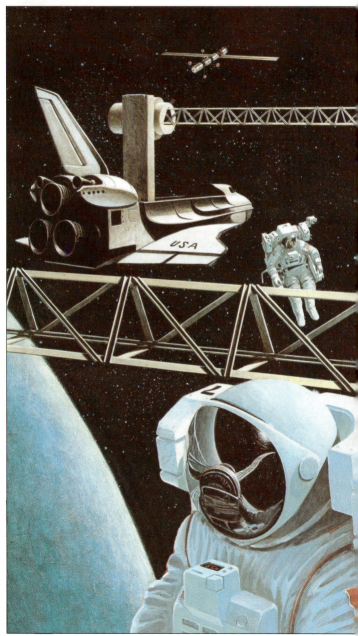

Soon, in factories in space, new metals will be made. Refined outside the earth's atmosphere and without the pull of gravity, they will be totally pure.

Soon, too, remote-controlled submarines will mine under the sea. They will be able to collect rich ores from the ocean bed. Even today, people are finding ways to dig metals from the sea-bottom. Although metals like nickel and copper have not run out, they are becoming more and more difficult and expensive to mine on land. But there are still riches under the sea which have hardly begun to be tapped. If they are not wasted, they will be useful for ages to come.

Index

alchemists, 17
alloys, 11, 18, 28
aluminium, 25
armourers, 20
bellows, 13, 15, 21, 24
blast-furnaces, 24
bronze, 11-12
calcium, 7
casting, 10-11
characteristics, 7

clockmakers, 19
conductors, 7
copper, 9, 11, 18, 35
coppersmiths, 20
cutlers, 21
electricity, 7, 25
furnaces, 13, 24
gold, 9, 17-19
hallmarks, 18
iron, 7-17, 25-31

*Iron Age, 12
jewellers, 19, 21
lead, 17, 32
meteorites, 12
mining, 22-23, 35
moulding, 10-11
nickel, 18, 25, 35
ores, 9-10, 12-13
platinum, 19, 32
poisoning, 33*

*recycling, 32
scrap-metal, 32
silver, 9, 17-19
smiths, 15, 25
space, 35
steel, 27-30
steelworks, 28
titanium, 25
uranium, 25, 32*

Pocket Worlds – building up into a child's first encyclopaedia:

<u>The Natural World</u>
The Air Around Us
The Sunshine Around Us
The Moon and Stars Around Us
Our Blue Planet
Coast and Seashore
Mountains of the World
Volcanoes of the World
Deserts and Jungles
Rocks and Stones
In the Hedgerow
The Life of the Tree
Woodland and Forest
The Pond
Fruits of the Earth

<u>The Animal World</u>
Prehistoric Animals
The Long Life and Gentle Ways of the Elephant
Big Bears and Little Bears
Big Cats and Little Cats
Farm Animals Around the World
Cows and Their Cousins
All About Pigs
The Horse
Monkeys and Apes
Crocodiles and Alligators
Whales, Dolphins and Seals
Wolf!
Bees, Ants and Termites
Caterpillars, Butterflies and Moths
Birds and Their Nests
Wildlife Alert!
Wildlife in Towns
Animals in Winter
Animals on the Move
Animals Underground
Animal Architects
Animal Colours and Patterns
Teeth and Fangs

<u>The World of Food</u>
Chocolate, Tea and Coffee
Bread Around the World